OLD TESTAMENT CHARACTERS

12 STUDIES FOR INDIVIDUALS OR GROUPS

LifeGuide®
BIBLE STUDIES

PETER SCAZZERO

IVP Connect

An imprint of InterVarsity Press
Downers Grove, Illinois

InterVarsity Press
P.O. Box 1400, Downers Grove, IL 60515-1426
ivpress.com
email@ivpress.com

InterVarsity Press® is the book-publishing division of InterVarsity Christian Fellowship/USA®, a movement of students and faculty active on campus at hundreds of universities, colleges and schools of nursing in the United States of America, and a member movement of the International Fellowship of Evangelical Students. For information about local and regional activities, visit intervarsity.org.

LifeGuide® is a registered trademark of InterVarsity Christian Fellowship.

Cover photograph: © Maggie Brodie / Trevillion Images

ISBN 978-0-8308-3059-6

Printed in the United States of America ∞

g green press INITIATIVE *As a member of the Green Press Initiative, InterVarsity Press is committed to protecting the environment and to the responsible use of natural resources. To learn more, visit greenpressinitiative.org.*

P	30	29	28	27	26	25	24	23	22	21	20	19	18
Y	30	29	28	27	26	25	24	23	22	21	20	19	

Contents

Old Testament History at a Glance*

2000 B.C. _____ The Period of the Patriarchs: Abraham, Isaac, Jacob
Abraham

1700 B.C. _____ Slavery in Egypt

Moses

1280 B.C. _____ The Exodus from Egypt
Caleb and Joshua

1240 B.C. _____ The Conquest of the Promised Land
Achan

1220 B.C. _____ Period of the Judges
Deborah

Hannah
Samuel

1050 B.C. _____ Beginning of the Monarchy (United Kingdom)
Saul
David

---

931 B.C. _____ Division of the Monarchy (Divided Kingdom)

Elijah
Jonah (?)

---

722 B.C. _____ Fall of Samaria

---

586 B.C. _____ Fall of Jerusalem
Exile in Babylon
Daniel

---

538 B.C. _____ The Return from Exile
Esther

---

*The dates for the various characters (and events) are approximate. They do not cover the full lifespan of the characters but only the periods of time covered in the studies in this guide.

Getting the Most Out of
Old Testament Characters

We live in a world that is desperate for heroes. Supermacho film and TV stars, professional athletes, rock stars and "the rich and famous" are held up to us as role models. Yet deep within the pages of the Old Testament, we meet real, flesh-and-blood people like us, with both weaknesses and strengths, who provide us with genuine models we can imitate.

The problem, however, is that large portions of the Old Testament remain literally a closed book to many. The reason is not hard to find. The Old Testament is not a continuous, easy-to-read account of the history of Israel. In a collection of thirty-nine different books, written over a period of a thousand years, one encounters poetry, law, history, moral advice, prophecy and visions. Add to this the very different customs and cultures of these times and it becomes easy to see why many have become discouraged.

This guide has been written to help you open the Old Testament portion of God's revelation and to discover the buried treasures that lie within, deep and undiscovered. It is my hope that your understanding of the ways of our God will be significantly expanded as you work through these character studies.

The most surprising discovery made, however, by studying the lives of people such as Esther, Jonah, Elijah and Joshua is their humanness and relevance for today. As Jerry Sittser has written:

> We observe that God uses common people . . . to make history. The powerful of society often form a background in which the little people, the faithful people, honor God and transform the world. God loves to

use the unassuming, unimportant people in the world. He only requires us to say with Mary, "Let it be to me according to your word." (*The Adventure* [Downers Grove, Ill.: InterVarsity Press, 1985], p. 78.)

Toward this end, twelve inductive Bible studies have been prepared. Each study deals with a different biblical character, such as Hannah, Daniel or Moses, and a different theme relevant to our following Jesus today (prayer, temptation, lordship and so on). Although the studies are not arranged chronologically, a simple chart is provided on page 4 to help you understand where a particular character fits within the history of Israel. The leader's notes also answer many of the background questions that will inevitably arise. Feel free, of course, to change the order of the studies to meet your own particular needs.

It is my prayer that we might be better participants in the shaping of God's drama today by our careful reflection on the successes and failures of the men and women who have gone before us.

Therefore, since we are surrounded by such a great cloud of witnesses, let us throw off everything that hinders and the sin that so easily entangles, and let us run with perseverance the race marked out for us. (Hebrews 12:1)

Suggestions for Individual Study

1. As you begin each study, pray that God will speak to you through his Word.

2. Read the introduction to the study and respond to the personal reflection question or exercise. This is designed to help you focus on God and on the theme of the study.

3. Each study deals with a particular passage—so that you can delve into the author's meaning in that context. Read and reread the passage to be studied. If you are studying a book, it will be helpful to read through the entire book prior to the first study. The questions are written using the language of the New International Version, so you may wish to use that version of the Bible. The New Revised Standard

Version is also recommended.

4. This is an inductive Bible study, designed to help you discover for yourself what Scripture is saying. The study includes three types of questions. *Observation* questions ask about the basic facts: who, what, when, where and how. *Interpretation* questions delve into the meaning of the passage. *Application* questions help you discover the implications of the text for growing in Christ. These three keys unlock the treasures of Scripture.

Write your answers to the questions in the spaces provided or in a personal journal. Writing can bring clarity and deeper understanding of yourself and of God's Word.

5. It might be good to have a Bible dictionary handy. Use it to look up any unfamiliar words, names or places.

6. Use the prayer suggestion to guide you in thanking God for what you have learned and to pray about the applications that have come to mind.

7. You may want to go on to the suggestion under "Now or Later," or you may want to use that idea for your next study.

Suggestions for Members of a Group Study

1. Come to the study prepared. Follow the suggestions for individual study mentioned above. You will find that careful preparation will greatly enrich your time spent in group discussion.

2. Be willing to participate in the discussion. The leader of your group will not be lecturing. Instead, he or she will be encouraging the members of the group to discuss what they have learned. The leader will be asking the questions that are found in this guide.

3. Stick to the topic being discussed. Your answers should be based on the verses which are the focus of the discussion and not on outside authorities such as commentaries or speakers. These studies focus on a particular passage of Scripture. Only rarely should you refer to other portions of the Bible. This allows for everyone to participate in in-depth study on equal ground.

4. Be sensitive to the other members of the group. Listen attentively when they describe what they have learned. You may be surprised by their insights! Each question assumes a variety of answers. Many questions do not have "right" answers, particularly questions that aim at meaning or application. Instead the questions push us to explore the passage more thoroughly.

When possible, link what you say to the comments of others. Also, be affirming whenever you can. This will encourage some of the more hesitant members of the group to participate.

5. Be careful not to dominate the discussion. We are sometimes so eager to express our thoughts that we leave too little opportunity for others to respond. By all means participate! But allow others to also.

6. Expect God to teach you through the passage being discussed and through the other members of the group. Pray that you will have an enjoyable and profitable time together, but also that as a result of the study you will find ways that you can take action individually and/or as a group.

7. Remember that anything said in the group is considered confidential and should not be discussed outside the group unless specific permission is given to do so.

8. If you are the group leader, you will find additional suggestions at the back of the guide.

1

Jonah: Running from God

Sometimes we are reluctant to do God's will. We find it inconvenient. We are too busy. We feel uncomfortable. At such times we are tempted to ignore God and hope he goes away. When he doesn't disappear, we may even try to run from him.

GROUP DISCUSSION. Describe a few present-day scenarios of someone "running from God."

PERSONAL REFLECTION. Why are you sometimes reluctant to do God's will?

What false notions of God might play a part in your thinking?

Jonah had his own reasons for running from God's will. His experience challenges us to view our reluctance in a new light. Jonah, much like the people of Israel around him, had little compassion for the people of Nineveh, their enemies. Nonetheless God called him to move toward those he hated. *Read Jonah 1:1-16.*

1. What does God command Jonah to do and why (1:1-2)?

2. Nineveh, the capital of the Assyrian Empire, was the most feared and hated of Israel's oppressors. How does this help us to understand Jonah's response (1:3)?

3. When have you been tempted to run from God?

4. Tarshish (1:3), traditionally identified as Spain, was at the opposite end of the known world. Why do you think Jonah chose to go there?

5. What does Jonah's disobedience teach us about the nature of sin?

6. God sends a violent storm (v. 4) to block Jonah's rebellious flight. What effect does the storm have on the sailors and on Jonah (vv. 5-16)?

7. *Read Jonah 1:17—2:9.* Describe the terrifying sequence of events after Jonah was thrown overboard.

8. In what ways does God get your attention when you run away from him?

9. Why must we often sink so low before we have a change of heart?

10. *Read 2:10—3:3.* After being vomited onto dry land, how do you think Jonah felt when the word of the Lord came to him a second time?

11. In what ways has God "come to you a second time" in your life?

12. How does the portrait of God in these chapters encourage you to obey him?

Ask the Lord to forgive you for any areas in your life where you might be running from him. Affirm your commitment to obey him.

Now or Later

Read the parable of the talents found in Matthew 25:14-30. What additional insight does Jesus give for what it means to "run from God"?

2

Hannah: Praying in Pain

1 Samuel 1

Suffering and pain usually affect people's relationship with God in one of two ways. Sometimes we grow bitter or angry toward him for seemingly abandoning us and are tempted to "curse God and die" (Job 2:9). At other times our afflictions drive us to a new dependence and humility before God that deepens our walk with him.

GROUP DISCUSSION. When you are in suffering or pain, how do you react? Give an example.

PERSONAL REFLECTION. Have you ever felt like you were trapped in a hopeless situation? Explain.

For many years Hannah suffered the lonely pain of being unable to give birth in a culture where a woman's value was measured by her ability to bear children. From her we are able to learn how to pray in the midst of pain. *Read 1 Samuel 1.*

---

1. It is probable that Elkanah took a second wife because of Hannah's infertility. How do you think it made Hannah feel to live in the same home with the other wife and her children?

2. How did Peninnah add further pain and grief to Hannah each year when they went to Shiloh (vv. 3-7)?

3. Summarize the physical, emotional and spiritual effects of this ordeal on Hannah (vv. 7-8).

4. How might you have responded in Hannah's situation?

5. What does Hannah's prayer in verse 11 reveal about her desperation?

6. Why do you think God allows Hannah, and sometimes us, to reach such a point of despair?

7. How and why does Eli the priest respond to Hannah's intense prayer (vv. 12-14)?

How does he later serve as a channel of God's comfort and blessing to her (vv. 15-18)?

8. How does Hannah fulfill her vow to the Lord (vv. 20-28)?

Why would that have been difficult for her?

9. What crises and stresses are causing you to pray in pain at this time?

10. Hannah's son became the great prophet Samuel. How can her experience encourage you to persevere in prayer?

11. How have you seen God turn around a seemingly hopeless situation into great good?

Pray God would give you courage to trust him even when you can't fully understand what he is doing in your life.

Now or Later

Read Luke 18:1-8. What specific teaching on prayer does Jesus give from the parable of the persistent widow?

What else do you learn about the power of faithful prayer from the example of the widow?

3

Samuel: Hearing God's Voice

1 Samuel 3

Amid the hustle and bustle of daily life, we often find it hard to hear God's voice. Many "voices" shout for our attention—deadlines to meet, bills to pay, meetings to attend, phone calls to make, children to care for. We try to read our Bible but struggle to be still and to receive a word from God.

GROUP DISCUSSION. In what ways does God speak to us today?

PERSONAL REFLECTION. When is it hard for you to hear God?

In the days of Samuel few people were listening to God's voice. Politically and spiritually Israel was in terrible shape as they "had no king" and "everyone did as he saw fit" (Judges 21:25). In this study we observe Samuel as a young man, hearing the word of the Lord for the first time and beginning his prophetic ministry. *Read 1 Samuel 3.*

---

1. How do verses 1-3 set the stage for the events in this chapter?

2. Why do you think Samuel has difficulty distinguishing God's voice from Eli's (vv. 4-8)?

3. What do you think Samuel thought and felt as he listened to Eli and then returned to his bed (vv. 9-10)?

4. Why is the attitude "Speak, for your servant is listening" (v. 10) important in order to hear from God?

5. How does Samuel's openness to hear from God compare with yours?

6. What does God say to Samuel in verses 11-14?

7. Why would this have been particularly hard for Samuel to hear?

8. What is the greatest obstacle that prevents you from hearing God's voice?

9. What is he tempted to do with the vision (vv. 15, 17)?

10. When are you tempted to hide God's word from others? Explain.

11. How does Samuel's obedience affect his relationship to God and his future ministry (vv. 19-21)?

12. In what ways does Samuel provide an example for you in your relationship with God?

13. What practical steps can you take to be more attentive to God's voice?

Pray that God will open your spiritual ears and eyes to hear and see him.

Now or Later

Read Mark 1:21-39, noting a typical day in the life of Jesus. What was the key for him to hear the Father?

4

Abraham: Following God's Call

Genesis 12

Why am I alive? Where am I going? What does life add up to? Throughout our lives we feel a deep longing to understand our unique purpose—whether we are teenagers graduating from high school, college students contemplating careers, mothers with growing children, people at midlife or seniors in retirement.

GROUP DISCUSSION. What are some of the feelings and struggles you have as you think about being called by Jesus, to Jesus and for Jesus?

PERSONAL REFLECTION. What are one or two factors that hinder you from consistently trusting in God's promises?

Imagine that you are seventy-five years old and God tells you to leave your country, your way of life and your family to serve him in a place where no believer has ever visited. You do not have any friends in that country and must entrust yourself completely to God. Two more minor details: you will neither see the fruit of your labors nor return home alive. How would you respond? In Genesis 12 we observe God calling Abraham to such a mission. *Read Genesis 12.*

1. What does God command and promise Abram (vv. 1-3)?

2. Abram heard the call of God while he was serving other gods in Ur. What might have been his initial fears and reservations?

3. How did God's command to forsake all—country, people and family—require complete confidence in his promises?

4. God asked Abram to give up something great for something far greater. How is that also true in our experience as Christians?

5. Describe Abram's response to God's call (vv. 4-6).

6. Why do you think God reassured Abram in Canaan (v. 7)?

7. What are some ways that God "appears" to you (encourages you) as you follow him?

8. What effect does the famine appear to have on Abram (v. 10)?

9. What sins does Abram commit in verses 11-16?

10. How do crises and negative circumstances tend to affect your faith in and obedience to God? (Give an example, if possible.)

11. How does God intervene to put Abram back on track (vv. 17-20)?

12. In light of Abram's place in God's plan of salvation, what might have been the consequences if he had lost sight of God's call and remained in Egypt?

13. How might your obedience, or lack of it, have far-reaching implications in the lives of those around you?

Pray God would give you courage to follow the unique path and direction he has laid out for you.

Now or Later

Meditate on Colossians 3:23. How would your life be different if you did "whatever you do" for the Lord, and not for others?

5

Caleb & Joshua: Overcoming the Impossible

God seems to delight in setting up impossible situations—David against Goliath, Gideon with 300 men going into battle against 135,000 Midianites, eleven fearful apostles taking on the Roman Empire with the gospel. In the midst of a society that values control, power, security and human strength, it is no wonder we struggle to allow Christ to be formed in us through seemingly impossible situations.

GROUP DISCUSSION. How do you respond when confronted with a seemingly impossible situation?

PERSONAL REFLECTION. What impossible situation are you facing today?

The people of Israel felt that way after the twelve spies, whom Moses had sent out to explore the Promised Land, returned with their report. God had already freed Israel from their miserable slavery in Egypt and had miraculously provided for them in the desert. Now he asked them to trust him by invading the Promised Land. The problem, however, was that the land had large, well-fortified cities and was filled with giants. It seemed impossible. *Read Numbers 13:26—14:10.*

---

1. What report do the spies give to Moses, Aaron and the Israelite community after forty days of spying out the land (13:26-29)?

---

2. How does Caleb's perspective differ from that of the majority (13:30)?

---

3. What further negative information do the rest of the spies mention to oppose Caleb (13:31-33)?

---

4. Describe how the people react to the differing perspectives (14:1-4, 10).

5. Why is the temptation so great for them to return to Egypt?

6. Imagine that you are one of the Israelites at the border of the land God promised to give you. What thoughts and feelings would you have as you listened to both sides of this debate?

7. How do Joshua and Caleb respond in the midst of the tremendous unbelief of the people (14:6-9)?

8. Why do they come to an entirely different conclusion than the other ten spies?

9. Due to their lack of faith in the promise and power of God, this generation of Israelites, except for Joshua and Caleb, never entered the Promised Land (Numbers 32:10-12). How does our lack of faith prevent us from experiencing God's blessing and power in our lives?

10. What are the "giants" confronting you today?

your church or fellowship group?

11. How can the example of Caleb and Joshua encourage you to trust God more fully in one seemingly impossible situation in your life? What specific step(s) can you take to follow their example in dealing with your "giants"?

Spend time praising God for who he is, and ask him to grant you the confidence and faith of Joshua and Caleb.

Now or Later

Read the story of David and Goliath in 1 Samuel 17. What additional insights does this passage provide for you in overcoming the impossible in your life?

6

Elijah: Knowing God's Power

1 Kings 18:16-40

Imagine yourself living in a country where everyone is following other gods or religions. There are no churches, no Bible studies, no fellowship, no Christian literature. As far as you know, you are the only Christian in the land. How would you respond?

GROUP DISCUSSION. Describe a specific situation where you found yourself standing alone for Jesus. How did you feel and respond?

PERSONAL REFLECTION. How would you feel if every Christian abandoned the faith and you had to stand alone in your commitment to Jesus? Explain.

The prophet Elijah faced enormous odds. Israel had abandoned the Lord for another god, Baal. They had rejected Elijah in favor of the 450 prophets of Baal. Yet in spite of these odds, Elijah challenges Baal and his prophets to a contest with God. *Read 1 Kings 18:16-40.*

---

1. What do you learn about Elijah from this passage?

2. Why do you think Ahab agrees to a contest in verse 19?

3. What is Elijah's challenge to the people of Israel (vv. 20-21)?

What does their failure to answer indicate?

4. Israel was an agrarian society dependent on rain for its survival. Baal was the god who supposedly controlled the weather. How does this help to explain why it was so difficult for the Israelites to completely abandon Baal and trust solely in God?

5. In what ways are you or the people around you wavering between two gods?

6. Describe the conditions of the contest on Mount Carmel (vv. 22-26).

7. What is pathetic about the frenzied activities of Baal's prophets and their taunts of Elijah (vv. 26-29)?

8. What do Elijah's actions indicate about his knowledge of God's reality and power (vv. 30-37)?

9. Summarize the dramatic outcome of the contest between Elijah and the prophets of Baal (vv. 38-40).

10. What are the "Mount Carmel" situations you face? (For example, at work, at school, in your family or neighborhood.)

In what ways are God's power and reality challenged there?

11. How can you, like Elijah, rely on God's power in that situation? (Take into account what your part and God's part might be.)

Spend time in prayer, commiting your situation into God's powerful care.

Now or Later

Make a list of every situation where you feel weak today. Then read 2 Corinthians 12:7-10 for further insight into how God's power can flow through us.

7

Achan: Sin in the Community

Joshua 7

The effect of individual sin unleashed in the body of Christ can have devastating consequences. It can creep slowly through the life of a church, university fellowship, small group or Sunday-school class, quenching the work of the Holy Spirit and hindering the advance of God's kingdom.

GROUP DISCUSSION. Where have you seen the negative effects of one individual's actions in an organization, family, workplace or neighborhood?

PERSONAL REFLECTION. In what ways have you met God or grown spiritually through your involvement in the body of Christ?

Israel discovered the deadly, far-reaching effect of individual sin during its conquest of Canaan around 1300 B.C. In the midst of a miraculous victory at Jericho (Joshua 6), Achan took several items that were to be devoted to the Lord. Israel experienced the consequences of his sin in their next battle against the smaller city of Ai. *Read Joshua 7.*

1. Retell the story in your own words.

2. What happens to Joshua and the Israelites when they attempt to conquer the city of Ai, and why (vv. 1-5)?

3. After their defeat, the hearts of the Israelites "melted and became like water" (v. 5). Imagine that you are a reporter observing the scene. Describe the different types of reactions you might hear. (Remember, they do not yet know the reason for their defeat.)

4. When you or an individual in your fellowship or church experience a setback, how do you respond?

5. Describe Joshua's fears in your own words (vv. 6-9).

6. How does God respond to Joshua's pleas (vv. 10-15)?

7. Why do you think God held all of Israel responsible for the sin of one person?

8. What was the root cause of Achan's sin against God?

9. What sins or obstacles might be preventing your church or fellowship from progressing according to God's plan?

10. In obedience to God, Israel took radical steps to remedy the situation (vv. 22-26). What guidelines did Jesus give us in Matthew 18:15-17 to maintain holiness in the church?

11. What practical steps can you take to build up your fellowship or church this week?

Joshua 8:1-29 recounts how God granted the Israelites victory over Ai in their second attempt to conquer the city. Ask God to make you clean vessels through whom he can do mighty works.

Now or Later

Read Ephesians 4:17—5:7. What type of behavior do you most need to put off and put on?

What work does God need to do in your heart?

8

King Saul: Doing Almost All of God's Will

1 Samuel 15:1-23

We have an amazing capacity for self-deception. The first step of every twelve-step program is to come out of denial and to recognize one is powerless over the addiction. Jesus spent much of his ministry attempting to show the religious leaders of his day their hypocrisy and pretense (Matthew 23).

GROUP DISCUSSION. Why do you think we often settle for doing only part of God's will?

PERSONAL REFLECTION. In what area(s) of your life do you struggle with denial or self-deception?

Perhaps one of the cleverest schemes of the enemy is to convince us that doing *most* of God's will is enough and that by doing it we will receive God's blessings. King Saul fell into such a temptation. Instructed by God to fight and destroy the Amalekites, he succumbed to the wishes of his fighting men and did only part of God's command. *Read 1 Samuel 15:1-23.*

1. What message from the Lord does Samuel deliver to Saul, and why (vv. 1-3)?

2. How does Saul begin to obey God but later change his mind (vv. 4-9)?

3. What factors probably contributed to Saul's unwillingness to carry out God's explicit command (v. 12)?

4. Why is it so difficult for Saul to realize the seriousness of his sin against God (vv. 20-21)?

5. How does Samuel describe Saul's disobedience (vv. 22-23)?

6. Why do you think God equates disobedience with idolatry?

7. How does this description differ from the way we view our sin when we do not do all of God's will?

8. What "burnt offerings" and "sacrifices" do we sometimes offer to compensate for our lack of obedience?

9. What do you learn about the character of God from this passage (vv. 10-11, 22-23)?

10. What difference should these things make in our conduct or attitude when we are tempted to carry out only part of God's command?

11. Identify one area where you have been content to do almost all of God's will. What steps should you take to complete your obedience to God?

Pray God would give you a humble heart to seek and to obey all of God's commands.

Now or Later

Reflect on the beatitudes in Matthew 5:3-10. How do they differ from the heart of Saul as seen in 1 Samuel 15?

Which beatitudes, in particular, do you need to ask God to work into your heart?

9

Daniel: Tempted to Compromise

Daniel 1

In A.D. 156 a hostile Roman ruler threatened to burn Bishop Polycarp at the stake unless he renounced his faith. Few of us today face this kind of temptation to deny Christ. Yet our daily temptations to compromise our commitment to Jesus are just as serious. The seemingly small decisions we make carry with them far-reaching consequences both in our lives and in the lives of those around us.

GROUP DISCUSSION. When is compromise good and when is it bad?

PERSONAL REFLECTION. List three to four temptations you are presently facing.

Daniel confronted one of these "small" temptations. Having been forcibly exiled to Babylon, he was offered a prestigious education in the best school in the country. The problem, however, was that this once-in-a-lifetime opportunity also required a small compromise. *Read Daniel 1.*

---

1. Why were Daniel and his friends brought to Babylon and selected to enter the king's service (vv. 1-4)?

2. What tactics were used not only to train these young men but also to help them blend into Babylonian culture (vv. 4-7)?

3. In what ways are we pressured to conform to our surrounding culture?

4. Daniel and his companions accept the education offered by Nebuchadnezzar, the possibility of attaining top positions in the pagan empire and new names (vv. 4-7). Why do you think they agreed to these things but refused the king's food (v. 8)?

5. Why might it have been easy for Daniel to rationalize this seemingly trivial compromise?

6. In what small ways are we tempted to compromise our lifestyle or beliefs?

7. What creative arrangement does Daniel make with the chief official and the Babylonian guard (vv. 8-14)?

How is his proposal an expression of his trust in God?

8. In what situations do people ask you to compromise your convictions or beliefs without realizing it?

What creative alternatives might you propose?

9. In what ways does God honor the trust and obedience of the four young men (vv. 15-20)?

10. What might have happened to Daniel and his future ministry if he had compromised here?

11. In what ways does our obedience in "the little things" have far-reaching implications in our service to Jesus?

12. How can Daniel's example help you respond to one temptation to compromise you are facing today?

Pray that God would give you wisdom and discernment to be in the world but not of the world (John 17:15).

Now or Later

In situations similar to Daniel's, Christians often go to one of two extremes. Some won't even attempt to cooperate with what they consider to be a pagan system. Others cooperate to the point of losing their distinctiveness. Why are both extremes counterproductive to our desire to be faithful witnesses to Christ?

10

Esther: Saying Yes to God

Esther 4

We often find it easy to obey God when there is little risk or cost involved. However, when God prompts us to speak to a stranger about Christ, to take an unpopular position on a moral issue or to take a step of faith into the unknown, we often become indecisive.

GROUP DISCUSSION. In what situations do you find it difficult to openly confess or obey Jesus?

PERSONAL REFLECTION. Think of the life situation in which God has placed you (where you live, marital status, occupation, family). Ask him to show you his purpose for your life.

Four centuries before Christ, Esther found herself at a fork in the road: she could offer herself as God's instrument or deny her identity as one of God's people. She was a young Jewish woman living in Susa, the capital of the Persian Empire, when the king deposed his queen. To find another queen, he held a beauty contest. Esther's cousin, Mordecai, convinced her to conceal her Jewish nationality and to enter the contest. She was declared the winner and made queen of Persia.

Trouble began when Haman was made the king's right-hand man, and he determined to massacre all the Jews in the empire because of Mordecai's refusal to bow down before him. He convinced the king to issue a royal edict and to fix a day on which all Jews would be annihilated. *Read Esther 4.*

1. How do Mordecai and the Jews in the provinces react to the edict of the king (vv. 1-3)?

2. What steps does Esther take to comfort Mordecai and understand his distress (vv. 4-5)?

3. Describe the message Mordecai gives to Esther through the king's servant Hathach (vv. 6-9).

4. Esther is reluctant to heed Mordecai's exhortation (vv. 10-11) because neither the king nor officials know she is a Jew. This could cost her both the throne and her life. When have you been asked to do something that involved personal risk or cost? Explain.

5. What arguments does Mordecai use to contend with Esther's hesitation to intervene on behalf of her people (vv. 12-14)?

6. What does verse 14 reveal about Mordecai's understanding of God?

How does he view Esther's hesitance to act?

7. Mordecai asked: "And who knows but that you have come to the royal position for such a time as this?" Where has God placed you at this particular time in your life?

What may be a few reasons for which God has placed you there? Explain.

8. How does Esther finally respond to Mordecai and ultimately to God (vv. 15-16)?

What kind of help did she need in order to obey God?

9. How does the support of Christians encourage you to say yes to God?

10. Esther is graciously received by the king and effectively intercedes on behalf of the Jews. How can her example encourage you to make better use of the opportunities God has given you?

Ask God to give you boldness to faithfully speak and live for him.

Now or Later

Read Acts 4:21-31. Study the prayer of the apostles as they faced threats and persecution. What can you learn from them?

11

David: Loving Your Enemy

1 Samuel 24

"I love my enemy. I love God. It's my next-door neighbor I can't stand!"

"He hurt me so much that I don't think I'll ever be able to forgive him."

"Of course I've dealt with my anger and resentment. I just can't stand to be in the same room with her."

GROUP DISCUSSION. What person, or type of person, do you find difficult to love? Explain.

PERSONAL REFLECTION. Paul says that without love our Christian lives amount to nothing (1 Corinthians 13). Jesus said the world will know he is risen by our love for one another (John 13:34-35). Ask God to fill you with his love for himself and for others.

It's difficult to love those who have hurt us deeply. Saul slandered and falsely accused David. He hated and feared him because God had anointed David to become king in his place (1 Samuel 16:1-13). In order to protect his power and position, Saul kept trying to kill David. In this chapter we observe David's response. *Read 1 Samuel 24.*

1. What aspects of David's character are revealed in this passage?

2. Saul had an overwhelming military advantage over David (compare 24:2 to 23:13). In spite of this, how does David suddenly have the opportunity to kill Saul (24:3-4)?

3. How do David's men interpret the circumstances (v. 4)?

4. If you were in David's position, why might you have been tempted to follow the counsel of your men?

5. Why do you think David is "conscience-stricken" after cutting off the corner of Saul's robe (vv. 5-6, 10)?

6. How can viewing our enemy from God's perspective enable us to have a change of heart like David's?

7. How does David's proper understanding of himself and of God's judgment set him free to love his enemy (vv. 8-15)?

How can a similar understanding help us love others more freely?

_____

8. Describe the powerful effect David's attitude and actions had on Saul (vv. 16-21).

_____

9. Identify one or two people who might be considered your enemies. Why is it hard to act lovingly or respectfully toward such people?

What practical steps can you take to serve as a channel of God's love to the person(s) you have identified?

Spend time praying that God will grant you freedom to love as David did.

Now or Later
Read the parable of the Good Samaritan in Luke 10:25-37. What further instructions does Jesus give us about loving our neighbors?

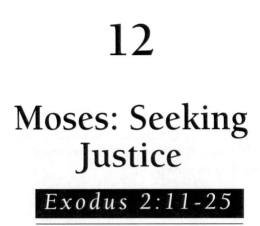

12

Moses: Seeking Justice

Exodus 2:11-25

War, racism, poverty, the denial of human rights—these are only a few of the bitter fruits of injustice that fill our world. Remedies to such complex problems have ranged from the nonviolent protests of Martin Luther King Jr. to the present-day insurgent movements in Latin America.

GROUP DISCUSSION. How do you respond when confronted with injustice?

PERSONAL REFLECTION. What issues of social justice move you to prayer or action today? Why?

Moses confronted the unjust social, political and economic system of Egypt. He had enjoyed the privileges of living in the pharaoh's palace since birth. Yet God placed within him a hatred for oppression and injustice. When he was forty years old, we observe him intervening to bring about justice for his people. *Read Exodus 2:11-25.*

---

1. What might have been some of Moses' feelings and motivations before, during and after the incident?

2. What does Moses do to try and help his fellow Jews (vv. 11-13)?

---

3. Despite his sensitivity to the injustice he witnessed, why is the particular action he takes wrong?

---

4. What mistakes have you made in a genuine effort to right a wrong?

---

5. Moses was raised in an environment of opulence, power and knowledge. What did it cost him to get involved?

What will be (or is) the cost for you to get involved with injustice?

6. How was he misunderstood by the very people he was trying to help (vv. 14-15; Acts 7:25-28)?

7. How does Moses again demonstrate an active concern for justice when he arrives in Midian (vv. 15-17)?

8. How does Reuel's reaction to Moses' aid contrast to that of the Hebrews?

What happens to Moses in Midian as a result (vv. 21-22)?

9. Moses spends the next forty years with the Midianites. Meanwhile the Israelites "groaned in their slavery" and cried for help. Describe God's response in verses 24-25.

10. Reflect on Moses' experiences in this chapter. How might each one have prepared him for leading God's people out of Egypt?

11. What experiences and training has God given you that could be used in the future for furthering his purposes?

12. There are many areas of injustice today: racism, neglect of the poor and needy, abortion. What one unjust situation might God be calling you to help change?

Pray that God will give you clear direction, courage and a sense of his timing.

Now or Later

Reflect on Jesus' teaching on the final judgment and how it relates to our involvement with the poor, the needy, the prisoner, the sick (see Matthew 25:31-46).

Leader's Notes

Leading a Bible discussion can be an enjoyable and rewarding experience. But it can also be *scary*—especially if you've never done it before. If this is your feeling, you're in good company. When God asked Moses to lead the Israelites out of Egypt, he replied, "O Lord, please send someone else to do it"! (Ex 4:13). It was the same with Solomon, Jeremiah and Timothy, but God helped these people in spite of their weaknesses, and he will help you as well.

You don't need to be an expert on the Bible or a trained teacher to lead a Bible discussion. The idea behind these inductive studies is that the leader guides group members to discover for themselves what the Bible has to say. This method of learning will allow group members to remember much more of what is said than a lecture would.

These studies are designed to be led easily. As a matter of fact, the flow of questions through the passage from observation to interpretation to application is so natural that you may feel that the studies lead themselves. This study guide is also flexible. You can use it with a variety of groups—student, professional, neighborhood or church groups. Each study takes forty-five to sixty minutes in a group setting.

There are some important facts to know about group dynamics and encouraging discussion. The suggestions listed below should enable you to effectively and enjoyably fulfill your role as leader.

Preparing for the Study

1. Ask God to help you understand and apply the passage in your own life. Unless this happens, you will not be prepared to lead others. Pray too for the various members of the group. Ask God to open your hearts to the message of his Word and motivate you to action.

2. Read the introduction to the entire guide to get an overview of the

entire book and the issues which will be explored.

3. As you begin each study, read and reread the assigned Bible passage to familiarize yourself with it.

4. This study guide is based on the New International Version of the Bible. It will help you and the group if you use this translation as the basis for your study and discussion.

5. Carefully work through each question in the study. Spend time in meditation and reflection as you consider how to respond.

6. Write your thoughts and responses in the space provided in the study guide. This will help you to express your understanding of the passage clearly.

7. It might help to have a Bible dictionary handy. Use it to look up any unfamiliar words, names or places. (For additional help on how to study a passage, see chapter five of *How to Lead a LifeGuide Bible Study,* InterVarsity Press.)

8. Consider how you can apply the Scripture to your life. Remember that the group will follow your lead in responding to the studies. They will not go any deeper than you do.

9. Once you have finished your own study of the passage, familiarize yourself with the leader's notes for the study you are leading. These are designed to help you in several ways. First, they tell you the purpose the study guide author had in mind when writing the study. Take time to think through how the study questions work together to accomplish that purpose. Second, the notes provide you with additional background information or suggestions on group dynamics for various questions. This information can be useful when people have difficulty understanding or answering a question. Third, the leader's notes can alert you to potential problems you may encounter during the study.

10. If you wish to remind yourself of anything mentioned in the leader's notes, make a note to yourself below that question in the study.

Leading the Study

1. Begin the study on time. Open with prayer, asking God to help the group to understand and apply the passage.

2. Be sure that everyone in your group has a study guide. Encourage the group to prepare beforehand for each discussion by reading the intro-

duction to the guide and by working through the questions in the study.

3. At the beginning of your first time together, explain that these studies are meant to be discussions, not lectures. Encourage the members of the group to participate. However, do not put pressure on those who may be hesitant to speak during the first few sessions. You may want to suggest the following guidelines to your group.

☐ Stick to the topic being discussed.

☐ Your responses should be based on the verses which are the focus of the discussion and not on outside authorities such as commentaries or speakers.

☐ These studies focus on a particular passage of Scripture. Only rarely should you refer to other portions of the Bible. This allows for everyone to participate in in-depth study on equal ground.

☐ Anything said in the group is considered confidential and will not be discussed outside the group unless specific permission is given to do so.

☐ We will listen attentively to each other and provide time for each person present to talk.

☐ We will pray for each other.

4. Have a group member read the introduction at the beginning of the discussion.

5. Every session begins with a group discussion question. The question or activity is meant to be used before the passage is read. The question introduces the theme of the study and encourages group members to begin to open up. Encourage as many members as possible to participate, and be ready to get the discussion going with your own response.

This section is designed to reveal where our thoughts or feelings need to be transformed by Scripture. That is why it is especially important not to read the passage before the discussion question is asked. The passage will tend to color the honest reactions people would otherwise give because they are, of course, supposed to think the way the Bible does.

You may want to supplement the group discussion question with an icebreaker to help people to get comfortable. See the community section of *Small Group Idea Book* for more ideas.

You also might want to use the personal reflection question with your group. Either allow a time of silence for people to respond individually or discuss it together.

6. Have a group member (or members if the passage is long) read

aloud the passage to be studied. Then give people several minutes to read the passage again silently so that they can take it all in.

7. Question 1 will generally be an overview question designed to briefly survey the passage. Encourage the group to look at the whole passage, but try to avoid getting sidetracked by questions or issues that will be addressed later in the study.

8. As you ask the questions, keep in mind that they are designed to be used just as they are written. You may simply read them aloud. Or you may prefer to express them in your own words.

There may be times when it is appropriate to deviate from the study guide. For example, a question may have already been answered. If so, move on to the next question. Or someone may raise an important question not covered in the guide. Take time to discuss it, but try to keep the group from going off on tangents.

9. Avoid answering your own questions. If necessary, repeat or rephrase them until they are clearly understood. Or point out something you read in the leader's notes to clarify the context or meaning. An eager group quickly becomes passive and silent if they think the leader will do most of the talking.

10. Don't be afraid of silence. People may need time to think about the question before formulating their answers.

11. Don't be content with just one answer. Ask, "What do the rest of you think?" or "Anything else?" until several people have given answers to the question.

12. Acknowledge all contributions. Try to be affirming whenever possible. Never reject an answer. If it is clearly off-base, ask, "Which verse led you to that conclusion?" or again, "What do the rest of you think?"

13. Don't expect every answer to be addressed to you, even though this will probably happen at first. As group members become more at ease, they will begin to truly interact with each other. This is one sign of healthy discussion.

14. Don't be afraid of controversy. It can be very stimulating. If you don't resolve an issue completely, don't be frustrated. Move on and keep it in mind for later. A subsequent study may solve the problem.

15. Periodically summarize what the group has said about the passage. This helps to draw together the various ideas mentioned and gives

continuity to the study. But don't preach.

16. At the end of the Bible discussion you may want to allow group members a time of quiet to work on an idea under "Now or Later." Then discuss what you experienced. Or you may want to encourage group members to work on these ideas between meetings. Give an opportunity during the session for people to talk about what they are learning.

17. Conclude your time together with conversational prayer, adapting the prayer suggestion at the end of the study to your group. Ask for God's help in following through on the commitments you've made.

18. End on time.

Many more suggestions and helps are found in *How to Lead a LifeGuide Bible Study*, which is part of the LifeGuide Bible Study series.

Components of Small Groups

A healthy small group should do more than study the Bible. There are four components to consider as you structure your time together.

Nurture. Small groups help us to grow in our knowledge and love of God. Bible study is the key to making this happen and is the foundation of your small group.

Community. Small groups are a great place to develop deep friendships with other Christians. Allow time for informal interaction before and after each study. Plan activities and games that will help you get to know each other. Spend time having fun together—going on a picnic or cooking dinner together.

Worship and prayer. Your study will be enhanced by spending time praising God together in prayer or song. Pray for each other's needs—and keep track of how God is answering prayer in your group. Ask God to help you to apply what you are learning in your study.

Outreach. Reaching out to others can be a practical way of applying what you are learning, and it will keep your group from becoming self-focused. Host a series of evangelistic discussions for your friends or neighbors. Clean up the yard of an elderly friend. Serve at a soup kitchen together, or spend a day working on a Habitat house.

Many more suggestions and helps in each of these areas are found in *Small Group Idea Book*. Information on building a small group can be found in *Small Group Leaders' Handbook* and *The Big Book on Small*

Groups (both from InterVarsity Press). Reading through one of these books would be worth your time.

Study 1. Jonah. Jonah 1:1—3:3.
Purpose: To realize the futility of running from God.
General note. Since the book of Jonah is short, you and the group may want to read through all of it before coming to the study.
Personal reflection. If you are leading a group and you'd like to spend a little more time warming up the group to the topic before the study, you may find that some of the personal reflection questions, such as those in this study, are useful as well.
Question 2. Nineveh, located on the eastern bank of the Tigris River in modern-day Iraq, was the powerful capital of the heathen Assyrian Empire. The Assyrians were the constant enemies of Israel. They frequently invaded Palestine, burning and looting cities, destroying the countryside and deporting its inhabitants.

The group should not assume that Jonah's only motive for running away was fear. Jonah 4 indicates that he also felt racial prejudice and religious hatred for the Assyrians. His attitude was entirely opposite of the Lord's. Jonah longed to see God destroy the Ninevites. God longed to have compassion on them and bring them to repentance. God's love and mercy toward the Ninevites (Gentiles) stands in sharp contrast to Jonah's (and Israel's) lack of love and compassion. While this is not the main point of this study, you may want to mention it to the group.
Question 4. Tarshish was located in the south of Spain, approximately three thousand miles in the opposite direction from Nineveh. It was as far west as ships were likely to sail from Palestine at that time.
Question 5. One way to look at Jonah's sin is that he is not just ignoring or avoiding God's will—he is going in the opposite direction!
Question 6. Jonah was by no means a coward. He deliberately chose death rather than letting others drown for his sin. He undoubtedly considered his fate just punishment for his sin. Note also that the Lord used this incident to demonstrate his power and sovereignty to the sailors, causing them to reckon seriously with Jonah's God—the God of Israel.
Question 7. Ask the group to reconstruct the sequence of events in the order they occurred. When we reconstruct his experience as it happened,

we find that he was hurled into the sea (2:3), waves and breakers swept over him (2:3), the waters engulfed him (2:5), he began to sink (2:6), seaweed wrapped around his head (2:5), his life was ebbing away (2:7), and at some point the great fish swallowed him (1:17).

Throughout this study, encourage the group to use their imaginations. Try to feel Jonah's fear when he is thrown overboard; see the seaweed wrapped around his head; taste the saltwater in his mouth; enter into his anguish at being banished from God's presence. This is a vivid story. Don't just analyze it; relive it!

Avoid speculating about the nature of the great fish and the possible significance of the three days. For a brief discussion of the literary nature of the book, see *The New Bible Commentary*, pages 746-47.

Question 12. It would be easy to assume that Jonah merely feared the Lord after being subjected to such severe discipline. However, Jonah realized that he deserved to die for his rebellion but that the Lord had graciously saved him and delivered him from death (2:2, 6, 8-9). Draw out these positive aspects of God's character.

Study 2. Hannah. 1 Samuel 1.
Purpose: To understand more deeply why and how to pray in the midst of suffering.

Group discussion. Help the group to be specific and honest. To help members of the group open up, you might want to be prepared to give one example of when you did not respond well to pain.

Question 1. You may want to note that there is no indication in the text that Hannah's infertility was a form of God's judgment on her.

Question 2. Elkanah made an annual trip to sacrifice at Shiloh, a city 18.5 miles north of Jerusalem, to fulfill the requirement that males appear three times a year before the Lord as part of a national festival (Ex 23:15-17; 34:18-24).

Question 8. Hannah consecrated Samuel to the service of God as a Nazarite. See Numbers 6:1-21 for the most complete biblical explanation of the Nazarite legislation.

In ancient times a woman nursed for as long as three years. We can imagine the difficulty carrying out this vow years later. Yet the Lord honored her faithfulness, and she later gave birth to three sons and two daughters (1 Sam 2:21). See Eccles 5:4-7 for the importance of keeping vows.

Questions 9-11. These are key application questions. Be sure to leave sufficient time to adequately answer them.

Study 3. Samuel. 1 Samuel 3.

Purpose: To learn to listen to God from Samuel's example, and to take practical steps to be quiet and open before him.

General note. The InterVarsity Press booklet *Meditative Prayer* by Richard Foster is a helpful introduction to this study and to the topic itself. You might read it before the study and recommend it to the group.

Question 1. "The word of the LORD was rare; there were not many visions" (v. 1). The spiritual life of the temple was in disarray due to the wickedness of Eli's two sons and Eli's failure to restrain them (read 1 Sam 2:12-26). Nonetheless, God was about to raise up a new prophet, Samuel, who would speak his words to Israel.

Question 2. Be careful not to get entangled in the question. The first part of verse 7, "Now Samuel did not yet know the LORD," is unclear since he did obey and acknowledge the Lord. The second part of 7 and verses 19-20 suggest that Samuel had not yet entered into the special relationship that he would later enjoy. (See Ralph Kline, *1 Samuel*, Word Biblical Commentary [Waco, Tex.: Word, 1983], pp. 32-33.)

Question 7. Samuel has lived his entire life in the temple with Eli. Eli served not only as his spiritual mentor but also was like a father to him.

Question 13. Many Christians through the centuries have found that keeping a journal is a practical way of learning to hear God's voice. A helpful introduction to journal-keeping is found in Gordon MacDonald's excellent book *Ordering Your Private World.*

Study 4. Abraham. Genesis 12.

Purpose: To consider seriously the importance of fulfilling God's purpose for our lives.

Question 1. You might mention to the group that Abraham's name was originally Abram, as is reflected in this passage. God changed Abram's name to Abraham in Genesis 17:5.

Question 2. See also Joshua 24:3 and Acts 7:2-7. You might use a map to give the group a sense of the distance involved. Be sure the group grasps that Abraham was probably surrounded by a totally pagan environment when God called him. It is doubtful that any of his friends or family encouraged him. Ur and Haran were centers of moon worship. Moreover, Terah, his father, seems to have lacked the vision and perseverance to continue from Ur to Canaan.

Questions 3 and 5. Hebrews 11:8 commends Abraham for obeying without any objection: "By faith Abraham, when called to go to a place he would later receive as his inheritance, obeyed and went, even though he did not know where he was going."

Question 11. God uses an unbeliever, Pharaoh, to rebuke Abraham for his disobedience and to place him once again in God's will.

Questions 12-13. Abraham's willingness to "looking forward to the city with foundations, whose architect and builder is God" (Heb 11:10) continues to affect people to this day. Help the group realize the large numbers of people they influence (or fail to influence) as a result of their obedience.

Study 5. Caleb & Joshua. Numbers 13:26—14:10.

Purpose: To understand the nature of faith and to be encouraged to trust God more fully.

General note. You will want to read all of chapters 13 and 14 before leading the study to gain a broader perspective on the story. Feel free to add details whenever you think they are appropriate.

Personal reflection. Consider health, finances, a difficult relationship, your family, a ministry opportunity, work and so on.

Question 2. Do not spend too much time on developing this point since in questions 7 and 8 the group will focus again on this crucial issue.

Question 4. Help the group see and feel the intensity of this rebellion. The people lose all faith and completely reject God's plan of redemption. They even consider replacing Moses with another leader—not one who will lead them forward to the Promised Land but back to Egypt!

Question 5. Imagination is crucial in gaining the full impact of the passage.

Questions 7-8. Joshua and Caleb were able to let go of sight and sense and fix their attention on the unseen reality of God and his promise. For them the obstacles were insignificant next to the greatness of the God of Israel (see Is 40:22). Since God had promised to give Israel the land and its inhabitants, Joshua and Caleb rejected the sin of unbelief committed by the majority and acted in faith. (See also Num 32:8-12.)

Question 9. The people of Israel did not want to enter the Promised Land, so God granted their request as judgment. They were forgiven for their rebellion but still were not permitted to enter the Promised Land (Num 14:13-25). God's judgment is sometimes that way for us.

Questions 10-11. Be sure to leave time for these application questions and for prayer.

Study 6. Elijah. 1 Kings 18:16-40.

Purpose: To understand how to apply God's power in our witness to the world.

Background note. Read 1 Kings 16:29—17:1; 18:1-2; and James 5:17 as preparation for this study. You might enjoy reading this passage dramatically. Assign various members of the group to read the parts of the narrator, Elijah, Ahab and the people.

Question 1. Ahab seems to be pleased with the opportunity to obliterate Elijah and the worship of the God of Israel once and for all. It was because of the God of Israel that the land had not seen rain for three years (1 Kings 17:1; 18:1)! The odds, 450 to 1, were in Ahab's favor.

Question 4. King Ahab's wife, Jezebel, was a Phoenician and a believer in Baal and Asherah. The god Baal was the "rider on the clouds," since he controlled the rain. The goddess Asherah was an ever-pregnant deity. People believed that when Baal and Asherah mated, the land would be fertile. God condemned Baal worship, yet it attracted Israel since it seemed to have worked well for the Canaanites.

Since it was a life-and-death situation for the Israelites, the logical thing was to worship both God and Baal. In this way they would be sure not to starve. We do the same things in many clever ways. We trust God for our future, our finances and so on, but just in case, we also trust in ourselves, other people and favorable circumstances. Help the group feel the tremendous attraction of Baal for the Israelites. This will help them apply the passage later on in the study.

Question 5. For example, wavering between materialism, personal desires or ambitions and the Lord Jesus Christ.

Question 7. The prophets of Baal took much of the day pleading with their god to answer. Their frenzied activities and self-mutilation were supposed to rouse Baal to action. Elijah had total confidence that Baal would not and could not answer.

Question 8. Elijah knew that God lives and, in contrast to other gods, answers the prayers of his people.

Study 7. Achan. Joshua 7.

Purpose: To examine our holiness before God as individuals and as a community of believers.

Background note. If you read Joshua 6—8 before the study, you will understand the context more fully and be able to answer background questions that might arise during the study.

Question 2. During the conquest of Jericho, Achan sinned by disregarding the command to keep away from "the devoted things" (Josh 6:17-19). In the conquest of Canaan it was the Lord who gave his people the victory.

> After the battle the people surrendered to Yahweh, as the victor, the fruits of the victory. Sometimes this spoil included men, women, children, cattle and possessions (Josh 6:17; 1 Sam 15:3). Sometimes these were all destroyed. At other times the women, the children and the beasts were spared. But the obligation was on Israel to surrender everything to Yahweh in recognition of the fact that the victory was his and that he had exclusive rights over the spoil, either to save it or to destroy it. (J. A. Thompson, *Deuteronomy* [Downers Grove, Ill.: InterVarsity Press, 1974], p. 128.)

Question 3. Remember that before this defeat Israel had conquered the much larger city of Jericho. The shock of defeat might be equivalent to United States or China being defeated by Costa Rica or Switzerland, two countries without standing armies.

Questions 7-8. Although Achan committed the sin, verses 1, 12 and 13 state that all Israel acted unfaithfully and broke the trust relationship between God and his people. This implies quite a bit about our solidarity and unity as the body of Christ. "If one part suffers, every part suffers with it; if one part is honored, every part rejoices with it" (1 Cor 12:26).

Question 10. "The wages of sin is death" (Rom 6:23). Achan received his wages *immediately,* as did a few other biblical characters (for example, Ananias and Sapphira in Acts 5, Uzzah in 2 Sam 6:6-8). Fortunately, God does not treat us as our sins deserve. He has poured out the punishment we deserve on Jesus, at the cross. Jesus died the death we should have died.

Jesus has, however, given us very clear guidelines for dealing with sin in the church. Be sure to read Matthew 18:15-17. Other biblical principles abound for living in holy community—for example, getting forgiveness (Mt 5:23-4) and giving forgiveness (Mt 18:21-35).

Study 8. King Saul. 1 Samuel 15:1-23.

Purpose: To understand the seriousness of disobedience, and to take practical steps to obey God totally.

Question 1. Shortly after leaving Egypt, the Israelites "weary and worn out" were attacked by the Amalekites (Ex 17:8-16). After God granted his people victory, he promised to completely destroy the Amalekites from the face of the earth (see also Deut 25:17-18). Now, through Saul, God determines to carry out his threat.

The command to "totally destroy everything," including women and children, presents a difficult moral and theological problem for the modern reader. You may what to mention three reasons for such a command. First, Israel was functioning as an instrument of God's judgment on a wicked, utterly sinful culture. Second, Israel needed to eliminate all forms of temptation that might corrupt and prevent them from being God's chosen instrument to the world. This drastic action was needed to maintain holiness (Deut 7:1-6; 20:16-18). Finally, in Hebrew the phrase "totally destroy" means "to devote to Yahweh." The spoils, then, were surrendered and dedicated to God and were in some way a sacrifice to God. (Read leader's note 2 in study 7). Be careful not to spend much time on this point.

Question 4. You may want to act out the dialogue between Saul and Samuel in verses 12-21, highlighting how Saul confidently boasts of having gone on the mission God commanded. Be sure the group understands how we often give similar excuses to God to justify our disobedience.

Questions 5-6. Samuel specifies the accusation in verse 22—what the Lord wants is not sacrifices and burnt offerings but obedience to his voice. He labels the disobedience as rebellion and equates it with the sin of divination and idolatry. Saul rejected the word of the Lord and as a result is rejected as king over Israel (vv. 22-23).

Question 7. Be sure the group grasps the way God views what we often consider "little sins." You may want to give an example from your own life to open up the discussion here.

Question 8. Obedience is said to be better than sacrifice in biblical texts such as Isaiah 1:10-11, Hosea 6:6 and Micah 6:6-8. You may need to help the group get specific here. For example, some people will give money to the church. Others will go out of their way to be extra nice. Still others may put on a mask of pity.

Although Saul finally confesses his sin in verse 24, his actions suggest that his repentance is not sincere. He only wants to be seen as repentant by the people (vv. 24-30).

Questions 10-11. Be sure to leave time for these two key application questions.

Study 9. Daniel. Daniel 1.

Purpose: To learn how we can respond to pressures to compromise our commitment to Jesus.

Question 1. The surrender and fall of Jerusalem occurred in three stages—in 605, 597 and 587 B.C. Daniel 1 refers to the first deportation in 605 B.C. (see 1 Kings 24:10—25:21). For a fuller discussion on the question of dating and history as it relates to the Babylonian exile, see Joyce Baldwin, *Daniel: An Introduction and Commentary* (Downers Grove, Ill.: InterVarsity Press, 1978), pp. 19-21, 77-79.

Question 3. Consider pressures we feel at work or school, among family or friends, with money and so on.

Question 4. Commentators give different explanations of why Daniel believed food from the royal table would have defiled him. (See Baldwin, *Daniel,* pp. 82-83 for a brief summary of the different views.) The crucial point, however, is that Daniel was convinced that in light of the exile, compromise on traditional food laws was unthinkable. It would have led them too far into conformity with the world that surrounded them.

Question 5. Remember that the overwhelming majority of Hebrew men in the school were eating the royal food. You may want to act out a dialogue between Daniel and two other Hebrew youths who were planning to eat the food. Imagination and creativity here can help the group grasp how powerful a temptation this was for Daniel. (Consider, for example, how unpopular he must have become!) Be sure the group understands the risks he was taking and what might have been the consequences.

Question 8. If you need an example to get started, consider the situation of being invited out to a bar by a coworker when what they really want is to develop a friendship with you.

Be sensitive to the different positions on lifestyle issues held by various members of your group. Although Scripture gives us clear commandments, it is not a law book. Often we must apply biblical principles to work out what it means to be *in* the world but not *of* the world. The apostle Paul gives helpful guidelines in Romans 14:1-23, 1 Corinthians 8:1-13 and 10:23-33.

Study 10. Esther. Esther 4.
Purpose: To reflect on how we can serve God in the situations that he has placed us.
Background note. If possible, encourage everyone in the group to read the whole book before the study to understand the context of the passage.
Question 2. Esther, apparently living in seclusion, is unaware of what has taken place until Mordecai sends her a copy of the edict, urging her to intercede with the king on her people's behalf.
Questions 5-6. Mordecai knew that God would not let his people be annihilated. If Esther did not speak out on their behalf, "relief and deliverance for the Jews will arise from another place" (v. 14). Verse 14 also indicates his understanding of God's sovereignty. These veiled references to God (God is not mentioned in the entire book) seem to be an intentional literary device to highlight God's continuing care and providence for the Jewish people, despite all efforts to destroy them. Thus, it was no accident that Esther was in a key position at this particular time. God had a plan for her to fulfill within his larger plan of redemption for his chosen people.
Question 7. God in his providence has placed us in a particular church or fellowship, family, neighborhood, job and country at a particular time in history because he desires to use us for the extension of his kingdom.
Question 8. Many commentators have noted that Esther's response was mixed. On the one hand she was unselfishly concerned about the fate of her own people. On the other hand, she seems to have been partly motivated by her own safety (4:13).

Nevertheless, she did allow herself to be used as an instrument of God.

Our motives, too, may be confused at times. We may not feel like model Christians, yet God, in his infinite grace and providence, desires to use us.

Study 11. David. 1 Samuel 24.

Purpose: To understand the biblical nature of unconditional love, and to take steps to show love to at least one other person.

Background note. Read 1 Samuel 15—23 as preparation for the study. This will provide the additional background information you need to help the group appreciate the fascinating relationship between Saul and David.

Question 2. Saul's army of three thousand "chosen" men were not only better trained than David's but also five times the size!

Question 3. David's men interpreted the situation as the Lord's doing and even paraphrased one of David's psalms to encourage him to kill Saul: "The face of the LORD is against those who do evil, to cut off the memory of them from the earth" (Ps 34:16).

Question 4. Help the group grasp David's "right" (humanly speaking) to get back at Saul. Hadn't Saul twice tried to pin him to the wall with his spear? Hadn't he sent him into battle with the Philistines, hoping he would be killed? Wasn't Saul out there with three thousand men trying to kill him and to thwart God's plans for his future ministry?

Question 5. Immediately after cutting off the edge of Saul's robe, David's conscience bothered him. He may have viewed his act as symbolic of snatching away the kingdom from Saul (see 1 Sam 15:27-28). Fortunately, his sensitive conscience would not let him continue. He quickly acknowledged his sin and forbade his men from harming Saul.

Question 8. Saul was overwhelmed by David's actions. He wept before him and confessed his wickedness. He even confessed publicly that he knew David was going to be king of Israel. Yet his repentance was not total. He did not give his royal throne to David on that day. Shortly thereafter, he renewed his pursuit of David with his army (see 1 Sam 26).

Question 9. Ask God for great sensitivity and wisdom as you discuss these final application questions. There may be some in the group who have been seriously scarred by others. They may simply need prayer so that they can forgive. Others may need to confess their selfish attitudes toward family or friends. Leave ample time to pray for one another.

Study 12. Moses. Exodus 2:11-25.

Purpose: To wrestle with the biblical response to injustice, and to take one step of action.

Background note. You should read Exodus 1:1—4:13; Acts 7:23-29, 35; and Hebrews 11:23-29 for important background information on this passage. Encourage the group to do the same before you meet together.

Question 1. "This phrase ['and watched them at their hard labor'] means more than 'to see'. It means 'to see with emotion', either satisfaction (Gn. 9:16) or, as here, with distress (Gn. 21:16). Moses is one who shares God's heart. God too has seen what the Egyptians are doing to the Israelites, and He will come to deliver (Ex. 3:7-8)" (R. Alan Cole, *Exodus* [Downers Grove, Ill.: InterVarsity Press, 1973], p. 59). Be sure to read Acts 7:23-29.

Do not be dogmatic here since the texts only give us indications. His feelings and motivations were probably mixed. He was clearly concerned with the issue of justice. The action he took, however, was clearly wrong. Try not to get bogged down in the theological question about the use of physical violence as a means of social change.

Notice that Moses had to act in secrecy because he had no authority. As a result, the Hebrew who was abusing his countryman challenged him: "Who made you a ruler over us?" Forty years later God sent Moses back to Egypt in his name and authority with clear instructions (see chapter 3). On that occasion God did deliver his people.

Question 5. See Acts 7:20-22.

Question 7. Note that Moses' active concern for justice went beyond the narrow bounds of his own nation and people.

Question 12. Be sensitive to what God is doing in the lives of various people in the group. God may be calling one person to get involved in some project immediately. He may have other priorities for another. The question of timing is very important.

Peter Scazzero, a former InterVarsity campus staff member, is senior pastor of New Life Fellowship Church in Queens, New York. He is the coauthor, with Andrea Sterk, of the LifeGuide® Bible studies Christian Character *and* Christian Disciplines.